# MOULE'S COUNTY MAPS

# THE NORTH OF ENGLAND

# ENGLANDS
# TOPOGRAPHER

or

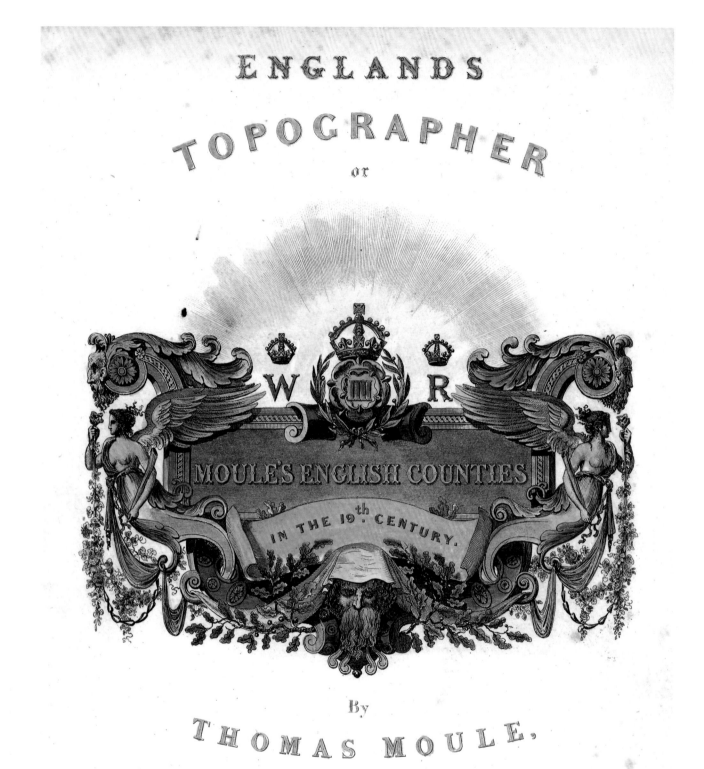

MOULE'S ENGLISH COUNTIES

IN THE 19th CENTURY.

By

## THOMAS MOULE,

*Author of Bibliotheca Heraldica & Editor of several popular Topographical Works.*

London,

Geo. Virtue, 26, Ivy Lane, Simpkin & Marshall, Stationers Court,

1836.

# MOULE'S COUNTY MAPS

# THE NORTH OF ENGLAND

## THOMAS MOULE

### Introduced by
### Ashley Baynton-Williams

THE
ENGLISH COUNTIES
Delineated by
THOMAS MOULE.

BRACKEN BOOKS

LONDON

PUBLISHER'S NOTE

The local descriptions accompanying the plates in this book have been
compiled from a variety of Victorian sources which
are listed in the Bibliography on page 48.

This edition published 1994 by Bracken Books, an imprint of Studio
Editions Ltd., Princess House, 50 Eastcastle Street,
London W1N 7AP, England.

ISBN 1 85891 194 X

Copy-edited by Christine O'Brien
Designed by Peter Champion and Paul Effeny

Printed and bound by Poligrafici Calderara S.p.a., Bologna, Italy

*Frontispiece, Decorative title-page and verso from* The English Counties
Delineated *by Thomas Moule, 1837.*

# CONTENTS

England and Wales *from* The English Counties Delineated *by Thomas Moule, 1837.*
*Coloured boundary lines clearly delineate the 52 counties of nineteenth-century England and Wales.*

# INTRODUCTION

Accustomed as the modern map-user is to the Ordnance Survey maps of the British Isles, we should nevertheless remember that they represent a relatively recent development in the cartographic history of these islands. When the Ordnance Survey was first undertaken in 1791, England already had a well-established tradition of regional map-making going back, in printed form, for 200 years. In contrast to the Ordnance Survey, the majority of these maps were constructed on a county-by-county basis, with over 100 different series of county atlases being published between 1579 and 1900.

During the last 80 years, as many of the traditional counties have been effaced from the map, there has been an increasing interest among private collectors in old maps that focus on each of the 52 counties that made up eighteenth-century England and Wales. Although every one of the different series has an individual claim to fame, among the most popular are the maps from Moule's *The English Counties Delineated*, published in 1837.

## MOULE'S COUNTY MAPS

Thomas Moule (1784–1851) was inspector of 'blind letters' (ones with illegible addresses) for the Post Office, but he was also a one-time bookseller, an author on English and Continental architecture and a contributor to William Westall's *Great Britain Illustrated*. A man of varied talents, Moule also wrote on the subjects of heraldry and genealogy. His modern reputation, however, was secured by his ambitious atlas of England.

In the face of this daunting undertaking, Moule chose to issue the atlas in parts, or more properly in monthly numbers. This was a common practice at the time, since it allowed publishers to recoup their costs as they went along and also spread the burden of payment for would-be purchasers. (Charles Dickens' novels were also issued in this fashion.) The monthly numbers were issued between 1830 and 1837, each with a map and a section of descriptive text relating to the county, written by Moule himself. Indeed, in the Preface, Moule claimed to have visited every county of England, except Derbyshire and Cornwall, when compiling the text.

In 1837, when the series was complete, the parts were bound together, and issued as *The English Counties Delineated*. Apart from the county maps, there were maps of the Isles of Wight, Man and Thanet, the environs of London, Bath and Bristol, Plymouth and Devonport and Portsmouth, a four-sheet map of the 'Inland Navigation', and plans of London, Bath, Boston in Lincolnshire, Oxford and Cambridge.

Moule's maps are celebrated as the last series of county maps to blend together both geographical and decorative features in their visual design so as to reflect the author's varied and fascinating interests. It seems as though every inch of the engraved area is utilized to full advantage, containing as it does the map itself, views of principal buildings, coats of arms and elaborate architectural borders. This happy blend explains the popularity this series has enjoyed both in its own day and among modern admirers and collectors. Then, as now, the maps speak of a rural paradise, of seamless continuity with the past, of prosperity, but above all of a sense of calm and stability.

Yet these very maps were issued in perhaps the most turbulent period in modern British history, as revolutionary change, and even revolution, beckoned. However much Moule's work seems to stand apart from this change, the enormous success that his atlas achieved was made possible by the technological advances in printing and publishing brought about by the Industrial Revolution.

At the beginning of the nineteenth century, printing plates were made from copper, the most widely used metal since 1477, when the first atlas was printed. Copper had the advantage of being relatively soft and so easy to engrave, but its softness made it susceptible to wear, particularly as great pressure was exerted during printing. A loss of clarity in the image could become visible after only a few hundred examples had been printed. Once this happened, the plate would have to be reworked to strengthen the engraved lines, a laborious process. In all, perhaps only 1,000, or at most 2,000 examples could be printed from one copper-plate. The new technology introduced paper-making machines, which could produce paper faster and more cheaply, while the earliest versions of the steam-press could print four times faster than the old hand-press. The effect of these innovations was to make printing far less expensive. All that was necessary was a more suitable printing plate.

In the 1820s the answer emerged: steel. Steel had the benefit of being both harder and more durable. Although it was more

Manchester and its Environs *from* Index-Gazetteer of the World...*published by John Tallis, c. 1855. A thriving industrial city, Manchester contained in 1857 some 363 textile mills and manufactories, 1,214 miscellaneous works and 1,743 warehouses.*

difficult to engrave, its durability meant that substantially more examples could be printed before the plate deteriorated – Moule claimed that 10,000 sets were subscribed for, although today only one, incomplete, set of the original parts survives.

While the roots of the Industrial Revolution lay in the eighteenth century, it was the first half of the nineteenth century that saw scientific discoveries transformed into tangible realities, as understanding turned into application. Perhaps the single greatest catalyst of change was James Watt's invention of the steam-engine, harnessing power for practical use. This discovery made possible the factory economy, but also led to the introduction and widespread development of the railway network, which provided a link between factories and the means of moving factory products to distribution centres.

## THE NORTHERN REGION

In medieval England, the focal point of the county was the county town which, in many cases, gave name to its county – for example, York, Lancaster, Derby, Lincoln, Nottingham and Durham. Within a predominantly agricultural economy, these towns were important as centres of distribution. But the transformation from a largely peasant-based agrarian economy into an industrial complex saw the emergence of new, industrial, urban areas, whose populations swelled as people faced with rural unemployment left the fields in their thousands to look for work.

York was one city of great eminence that found itself bypassed. In contrast, Sheffield, although long associated with iron smelting, was on the verge of ruin until the discovery of the South Yorkshire coalfield and the change from water-power to steam. From that time, the steel industry in Sheffield expanded rapidly, and the town's population almost doubled in the two decades between 1831 and 1851.

The role of the railways in the transformation of Britain cannot be overestimated. Use of rail freight enabled manufacturers to move their products quickly and cheaply to the customer, obviating the need for an industry to be close to its markets. Although this was a boon to all industries, it was of particular importance for farmers, for the railways allowed them to transport fresh produce further than ever before, and thus to reach much larger markets. Although he was not the first person to design and build a locomotive, George Stephenson's early engine built in 1818 provided the necessary means. On September 27 1825, the first passenger-carrying line in the world, the Stockton and Darlington Railway, was opened. This railway was soon followed by others, both in England and in Scotland, including the Liverpool and Manchester Railway, opened in September 1830, which was designed to carry not just produce and ores, but passengers as well.

Hand in hand with the Industrial Revolution went a rise in the general affluence of the population and an increase in leisure time. So, although the railway network was originally designed by companies for its application to commerce, it also enabled families to travel away on excursion trips, or even holidays. The most popular destinations lay on the coast; hence the rise of such northern resorts as Blackpool, Colwyn Bay and Bangor.

Just as some inland cities failed to benefit from the Industrial Revolution, so too did some of the ports. Bristol, the first seaport of England in the Middle Ages, saw itself superseded by Liverpool in the first half of the nineteenth century, partly as a consequence of the latter's better harbour facilities. Liverpool's development to a position of pre-eminence started with the construction of the wet dock, designed in 1709, which used floodgates to overcome the problems of the tide. This, the first of its kind in the world, much expanded the city's dock facilities. Liverpool also proved to be better sited for the trade with America than Bristol, and began to overhaul its rival, but its proximity to the new industrial regions of the Midlands and North confirmed the new order.

By a combination of native industry and good fortune, Britain led the rest of the world into the new industrial period, as the British work-force produced goods that markets in the rest of the world wished to buy. Thus, for example, in 1835 60 per cent of the cotton goods consumed in the world were pro-

duced in England and passed through England's docks to be enshipped for their destination. While, as we have said, Moule's maps have very much a sense of 'ancientness', he and his publishers were not slow to incorporate the geographical symbols of this new age – the railways and industrial canals that snake across the face of the map. In no county map is this more evident than in that of Lancashire. Successive additions of new railways to each map make a fascinating case-study for the collector of county maps or the railway enthusiast.

The charming historical documents collected in this volume provide a fascinating visual record of a bygone time. Although produced with modern technology, the maps retain an antiquarian feel; yet this same modern technology enabled their production in numbers large enough to make them readily available, and affordable, for the modern private collector.

Sheffield *from* Index-Gazetteer of the World...*published by John Tallis, c. 1855. Sheffield, in the West Riding of Yorkshire, expanded rapidly in the nineteenth century as a result of its successful steel industry and renowned silver plate.*

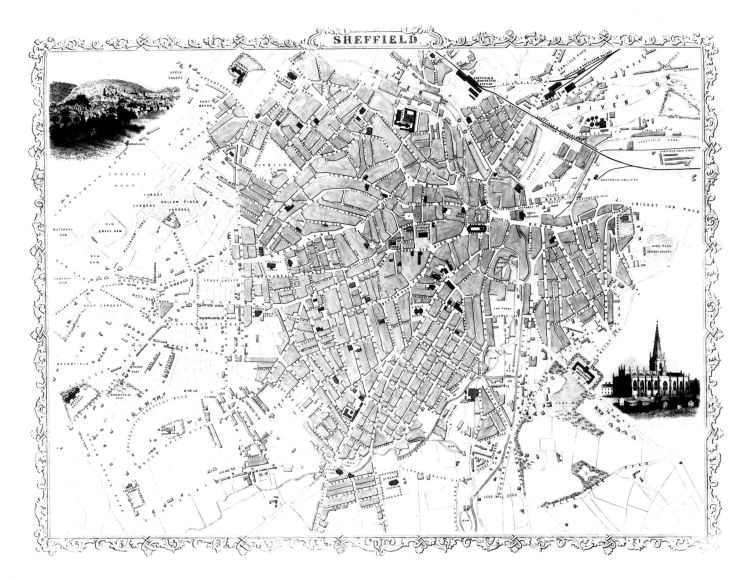

PLATE 1

# CUMBERLAND

## Thomas Moule

### *The English Counties Delineated,* 1837

A maritime county of England, Cumberland is bounded on the west by the Irish Sea and Solway Firth, on the north by Scotland, on the east by Northumberland, Durham and Westmoreland, and on the south-west and south by the sea and Lancashire. It is 58 miles in length, and its greatest breadth is about 45 miles. All but the north part of the county is very hilly, or even mountainous. Helvellyn, Skiddaw, Cross-Fell and some other heights exceed 3,000 feet. Amidst these mountains and hills are lakes of no great extent but of most romantic beauty. Among the rivers of Cumberland are the Eden, the Derwent and the Esk, some of which have in their course several noble waterfalls. There are mines of lead, copper, iron, and even of silver; but those of black-lead, or plumbago, are the most specific to the area. Coal, slate, limestone, granite and other building-stones also occur in various degrees of abundance. There is good pasturage even among the hills, and the arable land is fertile. Cumberland contains one city, two boroughs and 17 market towns, and has a population of 178,038. It returns nine representatives to Parliament.

## DERWENT-WATER

One of the most beautiful lakes of Cumberland, Derwent-Water is three miles in length and about a mile and a half in breadth. In this lake is seen the floating island, of which so many different accounts have been given by natural philosophers. Derwent-Water abounds with fish, and there are fine salmon in the season.

## CARLISLE

*For a description and town*

*plan of the city, see Plate 2, pages 12-13.*

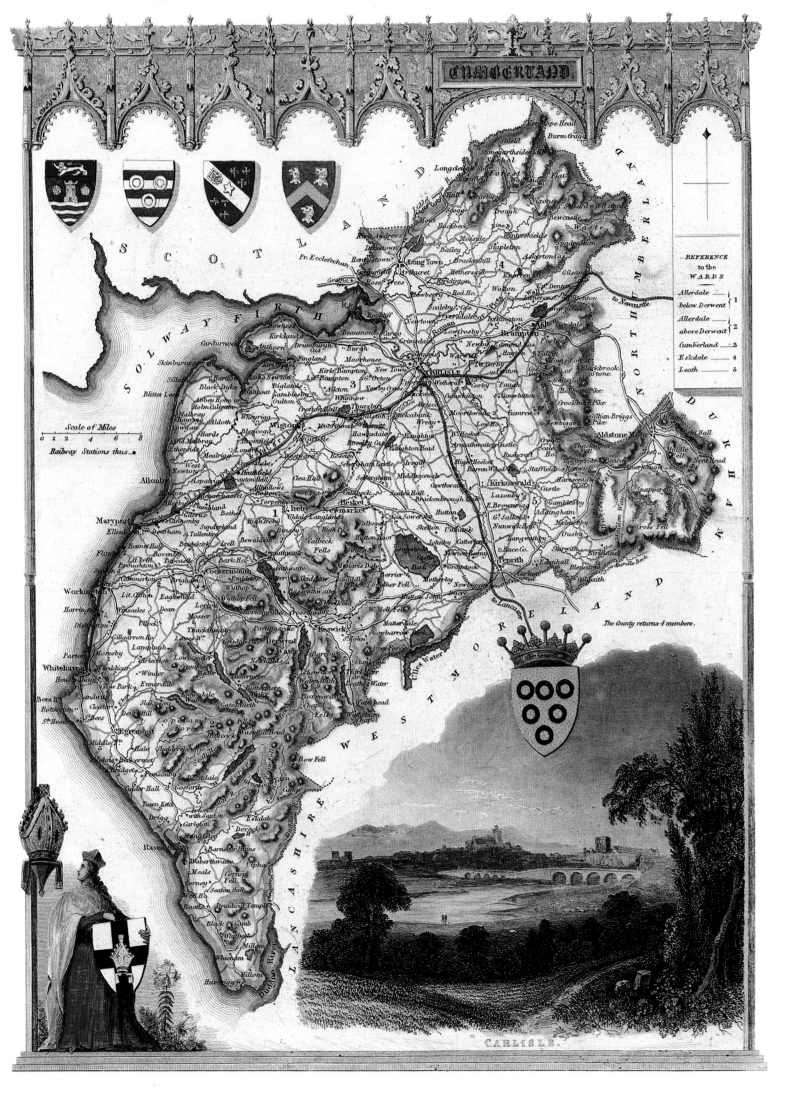

# CUMBERLAND

REFERENCE
to the
WARDS

Allerdale
below Derwent } 1

Allerdale
above Derwent } 2

Cumberland — 3

Eskdale — 4

Leath — 5

SCOTLAND

SOLWAY FIRTH

NORTHUMBERLAND

DURHAM

WESTMORELAND

LANCASHIRE

The County returns 4 members.

Scale of Miles
0 1 2 4 6 8

Railway Stations thus ▪

to Newcastle

to Lancaster

CARLISLE.

PLATE 2

# CARLISLE

## G. Cole and J. Roper

*The British Atlas: Comprising a Complete Set of
County Maps of England and Wales; with a General Map of
Navigable Rivers and Canals; and Plans of Cities and
Principal Towns,* 1801 and later.

Carlisle is an ancient city and the county town of Cumberland. It occupies a gentle eminence at the confluence of the Eden and Calder, 301 miles from London. The principal streets of Carlisle diverge from the market -place and are called English Street, Scotch Street and Castle Street, all of which are broad and spacious. The manufactured goods consist chiefly of cotton yarn, cotton ginghams and checks, Osnaburghs, drills, worsted shags, stamped cottons, superior hats, shamoy tanned-leather lindsays, nails, hardware, flax and ropes. The markets are abundantly supplied with provisions and excellent fish. Much business is also done at the various fairs, and during those held in August, for horned cattle and linen, and September for horses and horned cattle, all persons are free from arrest in this city, according to the terms of an ancient charter. Races are also held annually on a fine course on the south side of the Eden, the first King's Plate being given in 1763.

Nothing can be more pleasant than the vicinity of this city; the inhabitants with well-judged charity having employed a number of poor people during a dearth of employment to improve the roads and form handsome walks all around it. The population numbers 10,225.

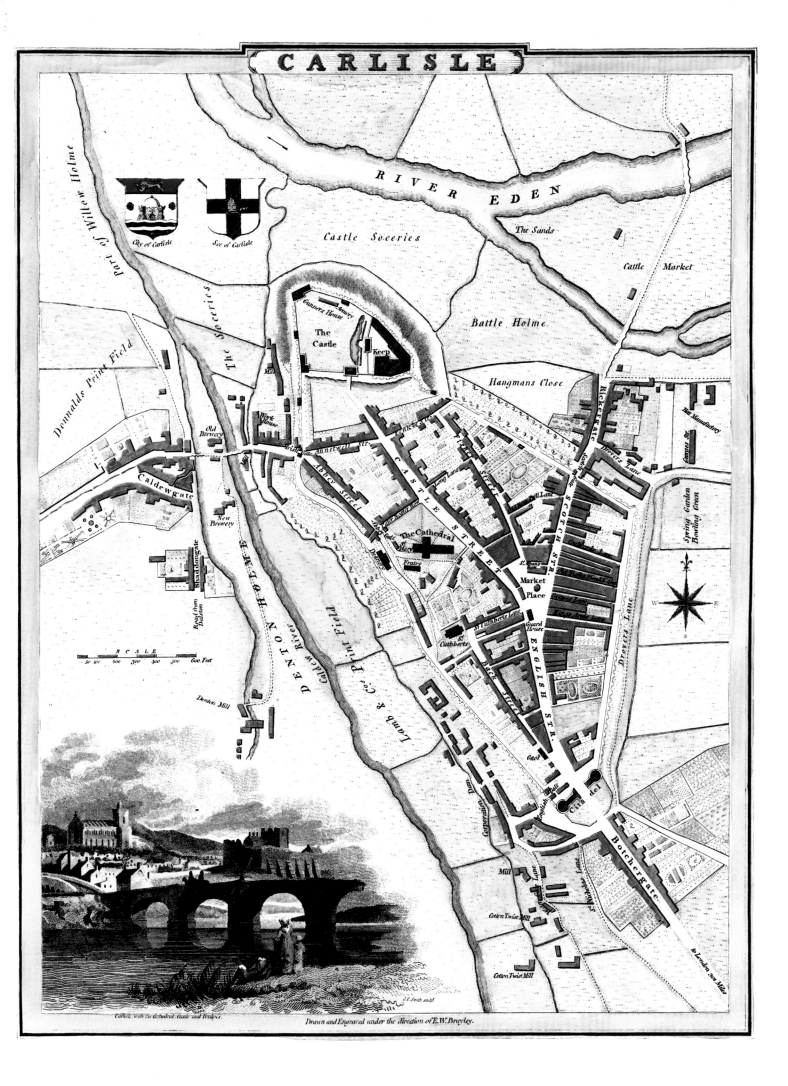

# CARLISLE

RIVER EDEN

City of Carlisle

See of Carlisle

Part of Willow Holme

Dennalds Print Field

The Societies

Castle Soceries

The Sands

Cattle Market

Battle Holme

Hangmans Close

Bickergate

Gunners House

Armory

The Castle

Keep

Mill

Work House

Old Brewery

Caldewgate

New Brewery

Shaddongate

Road from Dalston

SCALE
50 100 200 300 400 500 600 Feet

Denton Mill

DENTON HOLME

Caldew River

Lamb & Co.s Print Field

Abbey Street

Irish Gate

Annetwell Str.

Fish Gate

The Cathedral

Deanry

St Mary

Fratry

Water Master Lane

Fisher Street

Paternoster Row

CASTLE STREET

Long Lane

Lane

Maudsell Lane

SCOTCH STR.

Brewers Lane

Tan Manufactory

Lowes Str.

Spring Garden Bowling Green

W   E
S
N

Market Place

St Albans

St Cuthberts Lane

St Cuthberts

Back Street

Guard House

ENGLISH STR.

Gaol

Drovers Lane

Corporation Dam

English Gate

Citadel

Mill

Botchergate

Cotton Twist Mill

Cotton Twist Mill

to London 301 Miles

J.C.Smith sculpt.

Carlisle, with the Cathedral, Castle and Bridges.

Drawn and Engraved under the direction of E.W.Brayley.

PLATE 3

# NORTHUMBERLAND

## Thomas Moule

### *The English Counties Delineated,* 1837

The most northerly county of England, Northumberland lies next to Scotland, on the German Ocean, and is bounded by Durham and Cumberland. It extends about 70 miles in length and 50 in breadth, and contains 12 market towns and 460 parishes. The air is not so cold as might be imagined from the latitude in which it lies; and the snow seldom lies long, except on the tops of the hills, some of which are above 2,000 feet high. The soil is various; the eastern part being fruitful, having very good wheat and most sorts of corn, with rich meadows on the banks of the rivers; but the western part is generally barren, being mostly heathy and mountainous. The area yields lead and is one of the most productive and best coal-fields in England. Iron and glass-works are its principal manufactories; and it has some fisheries. This county is well watered by rivers, the principal of which are the Tyne, Tweed and Coquet. With a population of 250,278, Northumberland returns eight members to Parliament.

## ALNWICK

Alnwick is the county town of Northumberland and is 310 miles from London. Seated on the little river Alne, it is populous and well built. It has a fine market-square, surrounded with piazzas. One of the old gates is still standing. There is an ancient castle near it, the seat of the Duke of Northumberland. A market is held on Saturdays. The population numbers 6,626.

## NEWCASTLE UPON TYNE

*For a description and town*

*plan of the city, see Plate 4, pages 16-17.*

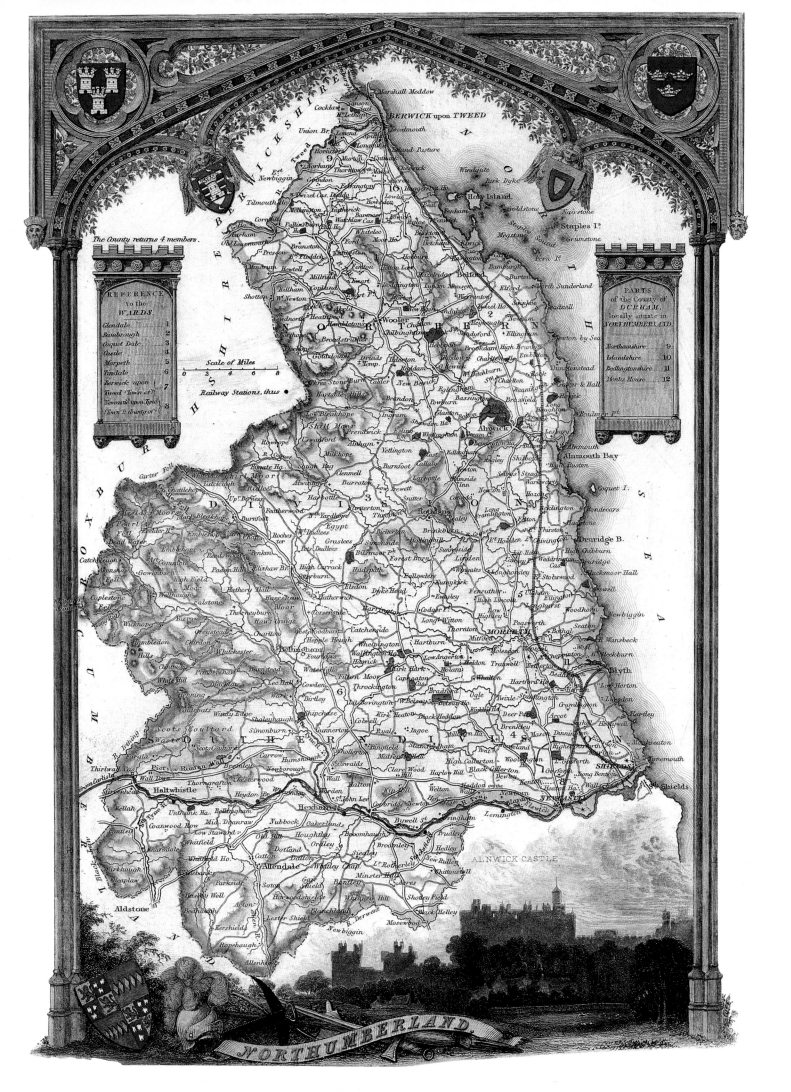

NORTHUMBERLAND.

ALNWICK CASTLE

The County returns 4 members.

REFERENCE
to the
WARDS.

Glendale ...... 1
Bambrough ...... 2
Coquet Dale ...... 3
Castle ...... 4
Morpeth ...... 5
Tindale ...... 6
Berwick upon ...... 7
Tweed Town of
Newcastle upon Tyne
Town & County of ...... 8

PARTS
of the County of
DURHAM,
locally situate in
NORTHUMBERLAND

Northamshire ...... 9
Islandshire ...... 10
Bedlingtonshire ...... 11
Monks House ...... 12

Scale of Miles
0 2 4 6 8

Railway Stations, thus ●

PLATE 4

# NEWCASTLE UPON TYNE AND GATESHEAD

## G. Cole and J. Roper

*The British Atlas: Comprising a Complete Set of
County Maps of England and Wales; with a General Map of
Navigable Rivers and Canals; and Plans of Cities
and Principal Towns, 1801 and later.*

The town of Newcastle occupies the north bank of the River Tyne over which there is a handsome stone bridge, connecting this place with Gateshead in the county of Durham. The town, including those parts outside the walls, extends about two miles along the banks of the Tyne, and one mile from the river-side towards the north and north-west; the ground being uneven but rising as it recedes from the river. The streets near the Tyne, which are the most ancient, are narrow, steep and irregular. The buildings on the declivity of the hill are extremely crowded. The bridge over the Tyne was erected in the place of a former bridge destroyed by the great inundation in November 1771. It extends 600 feet, consisting of nine elliptical arches, strongly constructed of stone, at a cost of more than £30,000, and completed in 1781.

The importance and prosperity of Newcastle have chiefly originated from the coal-trade, for the prosecution of which the town is admirably situated on the bank of a navigable river and in the midst of one of the most extensive coal-fields in Great Britain. The trade in coal between Newcastle and London was authorized by government in 1381. By 1699, two-thirds of the coal-trade of the kingdom belonged to this town, whence 300,000 chaldrons a year were sent to the metropolis. In 1811, the quantity of coal shipped from Newcastle was 634,371 chaldrons sent coast-wise and 18,054 overseas. Newcastle carries on trade with the south of Europe, whence are imported wines and fruits; with Norway and the Baltic for corn, iron, timber, hemp and other commodities; and about three ships are sent annually from this port to the Greenland fisheries. The principal exports from the River Tyne, besides coal, are lead, grindstones, salt, butter, tallow, salmon and a variety of manufactured articles. Newcastle is 301 miles from London. In 1811 its population was 27,587.

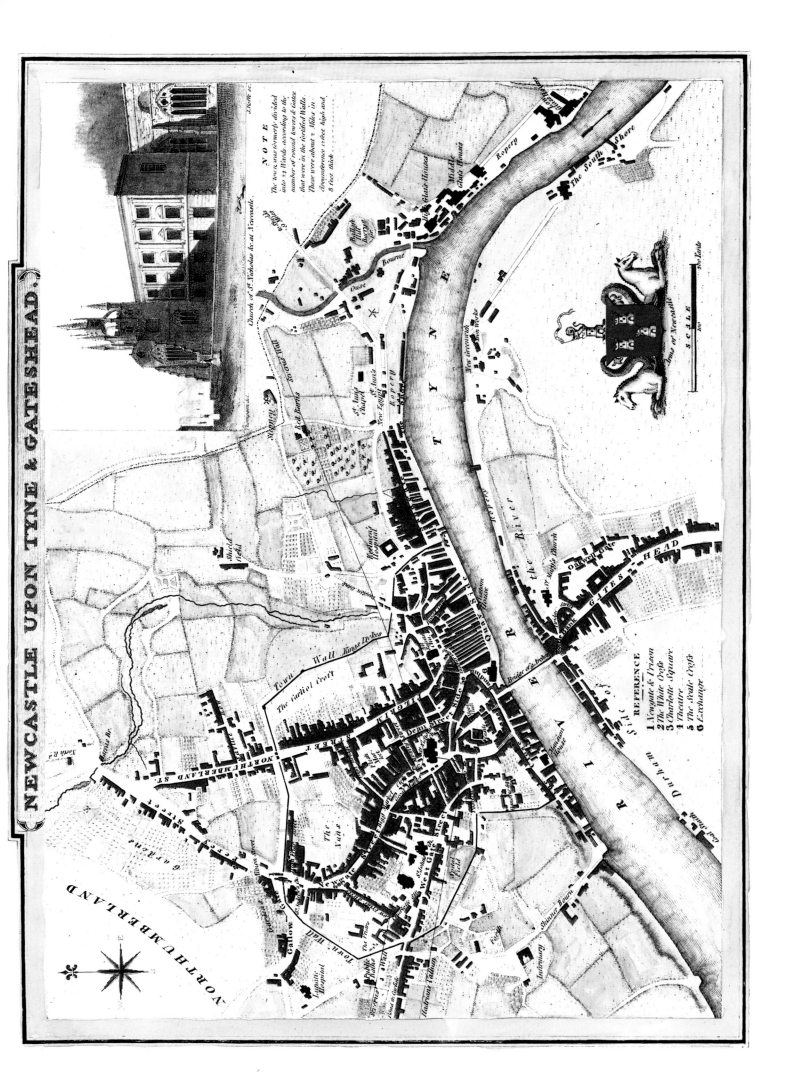

# NEWCASTLE UPON TYNE & GATESHEAD.

NORTHUMBERLAND

J. Roffe &c.

Church of St Nicholas &c. at Newcastle.

NOTE

The Town was formerly divided
into 24 Wards according to the
number of round towers & Gates
that were in the fortified Walls.
These were about 2 Miles in
Circumference 12 feet high and
8 feet thick

Arms of Newcastle

SCALE

TYNE

The South Shore

New Greenwich

Iron Works

Ropery

GATES HEAD

Oakwellgate

St Mary's Church

REFERENCE

1 Newgate & Prison
2 The White Cross
3 Charlotte Square
4 Theatre
5 The Scale Cross
6 Exchange

Durham

Side of

the River

Mansion House

Bridge of 9 Arches

Quay Side

Sandhill

NORTHUMBERLAND ST

Town Wall    Kings Dykes

The Carliol Croft

Gardens

The Nuns

Shield Field

Medical Hospital

St Ann's Chapel

New Road

Bourne

Ouse

Pandon

Byker

Red Barns

Severus Wall

Middle coal Houses

Michaelgate Houses

Bailiff Gate Quay

South R.

Lunatic Hospital

Public Baths

Hadrians Pallium

Infirmary

Skinner Bourne

Coal Staith

PLATE 5

# WESTMORELAND

## Thomas Moule
### *The English Counties Delineated,* 1837

The English county of Westmoreland measures 40 miles in length and 21 in breadth, and is bounded by Cumberland, Lancashire and Yorkshire. It contains 26 parishes and eight market towns. The air is very sharp and cold, but healthy. It is a mountainous area; two ridges, with peaks about 3,000 feet high, cross the county and run towards the sea to the south-west. There are some valleys fruitful in corn and pastures, and the hills serve to feed a great number of sheep. The principal rivers are the Eden, the Ken, the Loan, the Eamon, the Tees, the Lowther, the Hunna, the Winster, and the Lavennet-beck. There are also four lakes, called Ulles-water, Broad-water, Horns-water and Winander-water. The county yields coal, slate, building-stone and other valuable minerals. The principal town is Appleby, but Kendal is the most considerable for size, trade and population. The population of the county is 56,454. It sends three members to Parliament.

## APPLEBY

Almost surrounded by the river Eden, Appleby is the principal town of Westmoreland. It was formerly a Roman station, and there is a castle, the dungeon of which is very ancient. It is 266 miles from London. A market is held on Saturdays. The population is 2,519.

## KENDAL

Also called Kirby Candale (that is, a church in a valley), Kendal is the largest town in the county, and has long been noted for its woollen products, particularly knitted stockings, a thick stuff, called cottons, for the clothing of the people in the West Indies and for sailors' jackets, and linsey-woolsey. There is likewise a considerable tannery; and fish-hooks, waste silk and wool cards are manufactured here. The mills for scouring, fulling and friezing cloth, and for cutting and rasping dyeing-wood are well worth seeing. Kendal is pleasantly situated in a valley, among hills, upon the river Kent, or Kant, over which it has two stone bridges and one of wood, with a harbour for boats. The river communicates by a canal with all the late inland navigations. The town is 259 miles from London. A market is held on Saturdays. The population is 10,225.

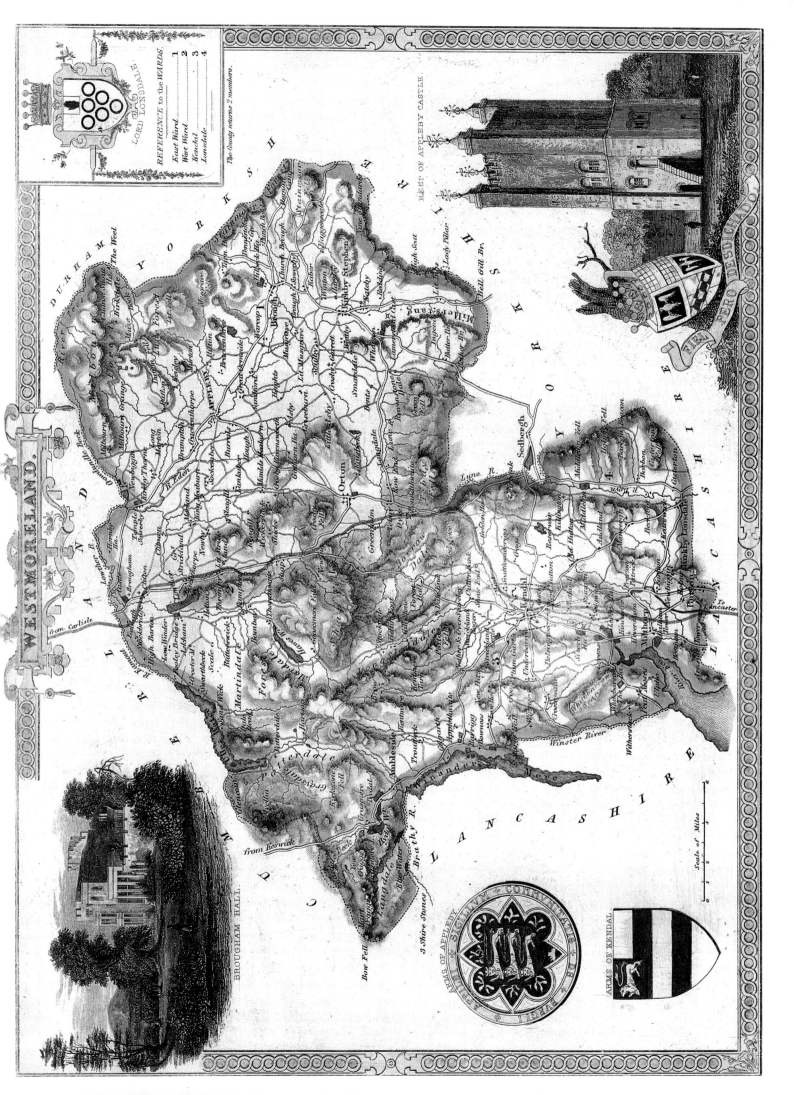

# WESTMORELAND.

LORD LONSDALE.

KEEP OF APPLEBY CASTLE.

FIEL · PERO · DESDICHADO

DURHAM

YORKSHIRE

from Carlisle

CUMBERLAND

LANCASHIRE

from Keswick

BROUGHAM HALL.

LANCASHIRE

3 Shire Stones

ARMS OF APPLEBY.

SIGILLVM ✦ COMMVNITATIS ✦ DE ✦ BYRGI ✦ APPELBY

ARMS OF KENDAL.

Scale of Miles

PLATE 6

# COUNTY DURHAM

## Thomas Moule

### *The English Counties Delineated,* 1837

A county of England, Durham lies on the German Ocean and is bounded by Northumberland, Cumberland, Westmoreland and Yorkshire. It is about 40 miles in length and 30 in breadth, and contains one city, eight market towns and 113 parishes. It is hilly, and some points are nearly 2,000 feet high. There are wide moors amongst the hills, and other tracts completely uncultivated. There are some islands on the coast, Holy Island being the largest. The coast is cliffy in some parts; other parts are shelving sands. The principal rivers are the Wear, the Tees, the Tyne and the Derwent. Coal, iron, lead, mill-stone grit and limestone are found here abundantly. The east and south parts of the county are fruitful in corn and pasture, and have a milder air than the other parts. Durham sends to other parts of the United Kingdom and to foreign countries both its native productions and the goods it manufactures, such as coarse woollen goods, sail-cloth, steel, glass, iron and so on. This county was formerly under the special jurisdiction of the Bishop of Durham as a Prince Palatine, but in 1836 the palatinate was vested in the crown. With a population of 342,284, it returns ten members to Parliament.

## HOLY ISLAND

This is a small island on the coast of Northumberland, one mile and a half from the nearest land. It is two miles and a quarter long and one in breadth, and consists of one continued plain. The soil is rocky; and the island has but one small town, or village, standing on a rising ground and consisting of a few scattered houses chiefly inhabited by fishermen. Under the castle, which stands at the southern point on an almost perpendicular rock nearly 60 feet high and accessible only by a pass cut out of the rock on its southern side, there is a commodious bay, or harbour, defended by a block-house. It has plenty of fish and fowl; the west part is left wholly to the rabbits; and there is not a tree on the island. The monastery, which covered nearly four acres, is entirely in ruins. The island is a peninsula at ebb-tide. It is 340 miles from London. The population is 809.

## DURHAM

*For a description and town*

*plan of the city, see Plate 7, pages 22–23.*

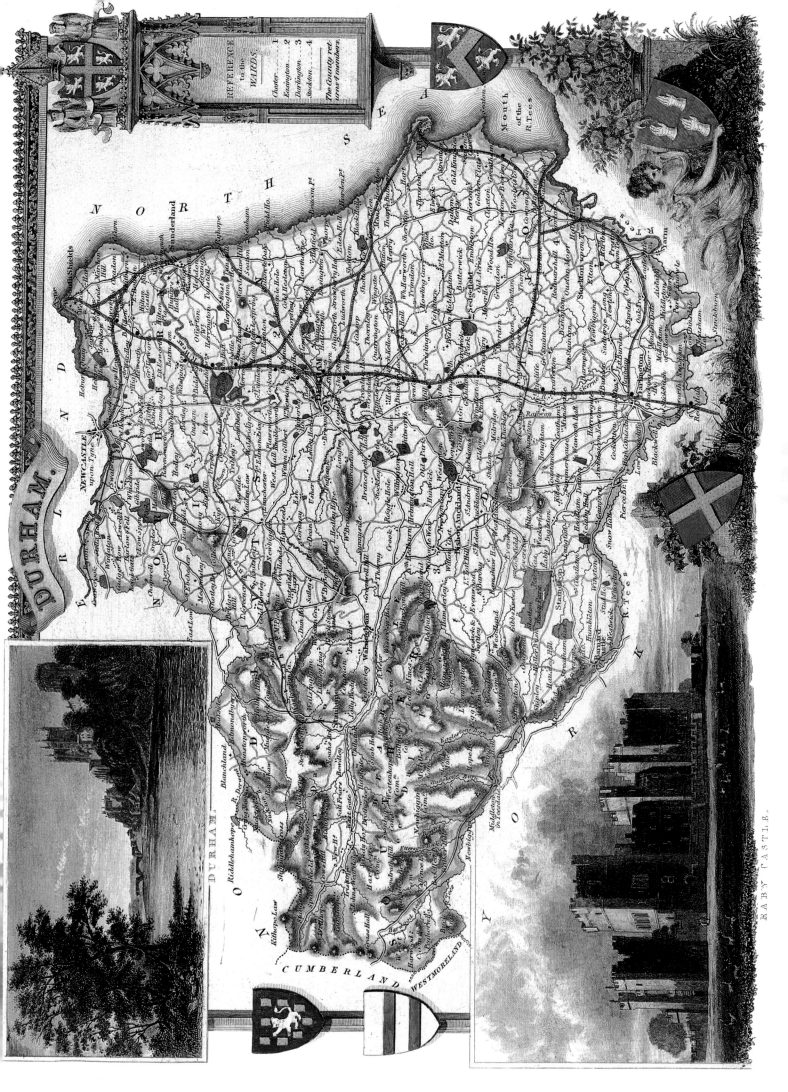

DURHAM.

NORTH SEA

REFERENCE
to the
WARDS.
Chester ............ 1
Easington ......... 2
Darlington ........ 3
Stockton ........... 4
The County returns 4 members.

Mouth of the R. Tees

R. Tees

DURHAM.

NORTHUMBERLAND

CUMBERLAND

WESTMORELAND

RABY CASTLE.

PLATE 7

# DURHAM

## G. Cole and J. Roper

*The British Atlas: Comprising a Complete Set of
County Maps of England and Wales; with a General Map of
Navigable Rivers and Canals; and Plans of Cities
and Principal Towns,* 1801 and later.

An ancient city, Durham is the county town of the county of the same name. It is irregularly built on a rocky eminence, almost encompassed by the River Wear. The highest ground in the centre is occupied by the cathedral and castle which, with the streets called The Baileys, are included within the limits of the old walls of the city.

The market-place is a small quadrangle, having in the centre a conduit to supply the inhabitants with water, on the south side a piazza where the corn market is held, and on the west the Guildhall. The central conduit is an octagon building, surmounted by a statue of Neptune, and the water is conveyed from a spring about half a mile distant. A new and handsome bridge over the Wear was erected between 1772 and 1777, at the expense of the Dean and Chapter. Durham is not distinguished for commerce or manufacture. Some years ago a woollen factory existed, which furnished employment for several hundred persons, but it has since been abandoned; and a cotton factory which had been established here was accidentally burnt down in January 1804, and has never been rebuilt. The city is 258 miles from London and has a population of 7,530.

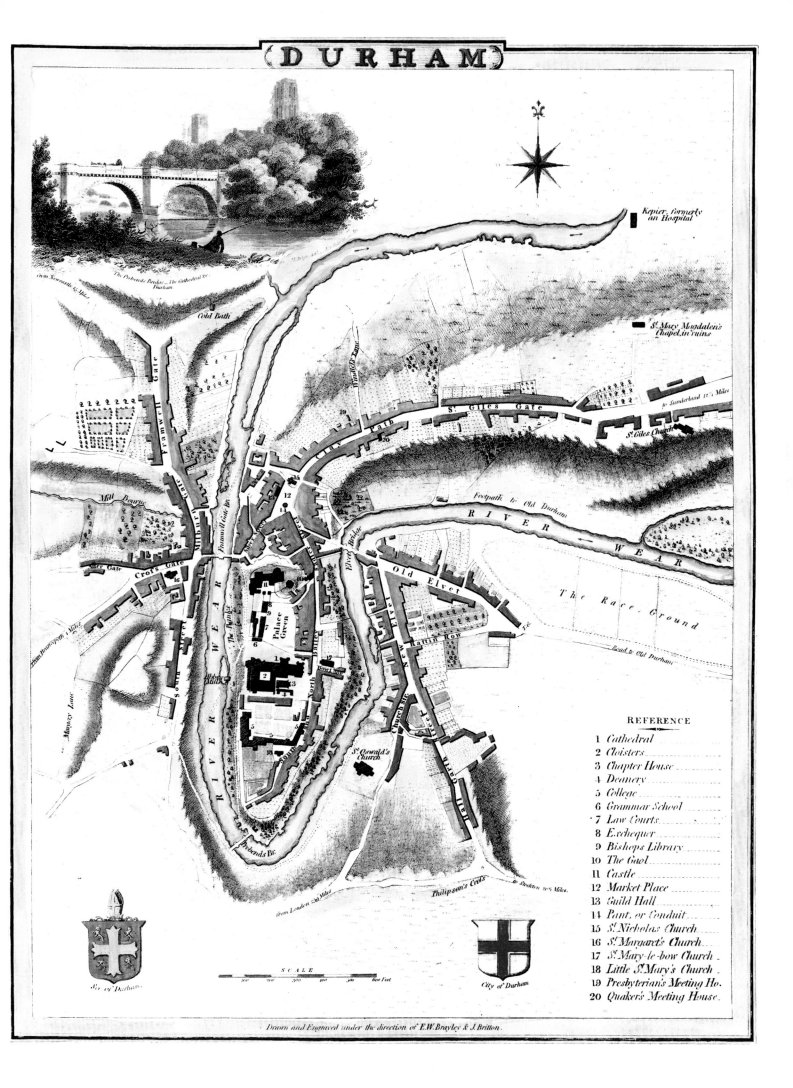

# DURHAM

The Prebends Bridge & the Cathedral &c. Durham.

Kepier, formerly an Hospital

St Mary Magdalen's Chapel, in ruins

St Giles Church

to Sunderland 12¼ Miles

St Giles Gate

Cold Bath

Mill Bourne

Alter Gate

Crofs Gate

from Brancepeth 4 Miles

Mavin's Lane

from London 262 Miles

Philipson's Crofs

to Stockton 20¼ Miles

Footpath to Old Durham

RIVER WEAR

The Race Ground

Road to Old Durham

Palace Green

St Oswald's Church

Elvet Bridge

Old Elvet

New Elvet

Church Str

Ratlin Row

Hally Garth

Prebends Br.

See of Durham

City of Durham

## REFERENCE

1 Cathedral
2 Cloisters
3 Chapter House
4 Deanery
5 College
6 Grammar School
7 Law Courts
8 Exchequer
9 Bishops Library
10 The Gaol
11 Castle
12 Market Place
13 Guild Hall
14 Pant, or Conduit
15 St Nicholas Church
16 St Margaret's Church
17 St Mary-le-bow Church
18 Little St Mary's Church
19 Presbyterian's Meeting Ho.
20 Quaker's Meeting House

SCALE
100 200 300 400 500 600 Feet

Drawn and Engraved under the direction of E.W. Brayley & J. Britton.

PLATE 8

# LANCASHIRE

## Thomas Moule

### *The English Counties Delineated,* 1837

A county of England, lying on the Irish Sea, Lancashire is bounded by Cumberland, Westmoreland, Yorkshire and Cheshire. It is 75 miles in length and 30 in breadth. It contains 27 market towns, 62 parishes and 894 villages. This county comprises a variety of soil and face of country; there being mountains of more than 2,000 feet high in the north and eastern parts, with wide moorlands or heaths amongst them; extensive bogs, which yield only turf for fuel and are very dangerous; and some most fertile land for agricultural purposes. It yields iron, coal, slate and other building-stones, salt and other minerals. Grazing is more attended to than agriculture. The fisheries, both in the rivers and the sea, are valuable. As a commercial and manufacturing county, Lancashire is distinguished beyond most others in the kingdom. Its principal products are linen, silk and cotton goods; fustians, counterpanes, Shalloons, baize, serges, tapes, small wares, hats, sailcloth, sacking, pins, iron goods and cast plate-glass. Of the commerce of this county it may suffice to observe that Liverpool is now the second port in the United Kingdom. The principal rivers are the Mersey, Irwell, Ribble, Lune, Leven, Wyre, Hodder, Roche, Duddon, Winster, Ken and Calder, and it has two considerable lakes, Windermere and Coniston Water. The population is 1,667,054. It returns 26 members to Parliament.

## LANCASTER

An ancient, well-built and improving town, Lancaster is the county town. On the summit of a hill stands the castle, which is not ancient, but large and strong, and now serves both as the shire house and the county gaol. On the top of this castle is a square tower called John of Gaunt's Chair, where there is a fine prospect of the mountains of Cumberland and of the course of the Lune, the view towards the sea extending to the Isle of Man. The town-hall is a handsome structure. Lancaster carries on some foreign trade, especially to the West Indies, America and the Baltic. The exports are hardware, woollen goods, candles and cabinet work, for the making of which last it is noted, and it also manufactures sail-cloth. The River Lune here forms a port for vessels of moderate size. Lancaster is 235 miles from London. Markets are held on Wednesdays and Saturdays, and one on every other Wednesday for cattle. The population is 24,707.

## LIVERPOOL

*For a description and town*

*plan of the city, see Plate 9, pages 26-27.*

# LANCASHIRE.

NELSON'S MONUMENT, LIVERPOOL.

## REFERENCES TO THE HUNDREDS.

| Northern Division | | Southern Division | |
|---|---|---|---|
| Armounderness | 1 | Lonsdale | 4 |
| Blackburn | 2 | Salford | 5 |
| Leyland | 3 | West Derby | 6 |

*The County returns 4 members.*

Scale of Miles
0 2 4 6 8 10

Railway Stations, thus ●

PLATE 9

# LIVERPOOL

## G. Cole and J. Roper

*The British Atlas: Comprising a Complete Set of County Maps of England and Wales; with a General Map of Navigable Rivers and Canals; and Plans of Cities and Principal Towns, 1801 and later.*

The whole town of Liverpool with its proper suburbs includes an area of 4,000 yards from north to south, and 2,500 yards from east to west. The latter side is bounded by the River Mersey, and on the opposite side are the borders of the townships of West Derby and Everton; whilst Toxteth Park skirts its southern side and the northern side joins the township of Kirkdale. The whole of this area, however, is not covered with buildings, though the practice of erecting new houses and forming new streets continues to prevail to an amazing extent; and, if persevered in, will in a short period occupy the whole space by a connected and spacious town.

Among the number of commercial towns in Great Britain it may safely be said that not one has so rapidly advanced to as great extent, and as great opulence, as that of Liverpool. From a small inconsiderable hamlet, this thriving sea-port, by the spirited industry, enterprising pursuits, and speculating habits of its chief inhabitants, has, within the last century, been singularly advanced in the scale of national importance. A history of Liverpool must be an account of the people not the place; for if the town be divested of its complicated traffic, increased shipping and nautical erections, it presents little else to recompense enquiry, or gratify curiosity. The present prosperity of Liverpool has evidently arisen from a combination of causes; and among these may be chiefly noticed its natural situation, its free water carriage with the numerous manufacturing towns and mines of the county, and the enlightened policy of its civil government. As the Liverpool docks were the first reservoirs and harbours, for the accommodation of merchandise, ever constructed in this country, it will be necessary to detail some further particulars. The wet docks are five in number: the Old Dock, the Salthouse Dock, George's Dock, King's Dock, Queen's Dock. These, augmented by five graving docks and three dry docks, presently occupy a space of about three miles in circumference.

In 1805, 4,618 ships with an aggregate tonnage of 464,482 tons were assessed for dock duties totalling £33,364 13s. 1d. Among the many and various articles of merchandise imported into the town in that year were cotton, coffee, sugar, tobacco, logs of mahogany and elephants' teeth. Before abolition, the slave trade formed the grand source of commercial enterprise here, and it has been stated that nearly two-thirds of the population were interested in the traffic of human beings; but their wealth and industry are now devoted to purposes more fitting to the promotion of national prosperity. Liverpool is 204 miles from London. In 1802 its population was 77,663.

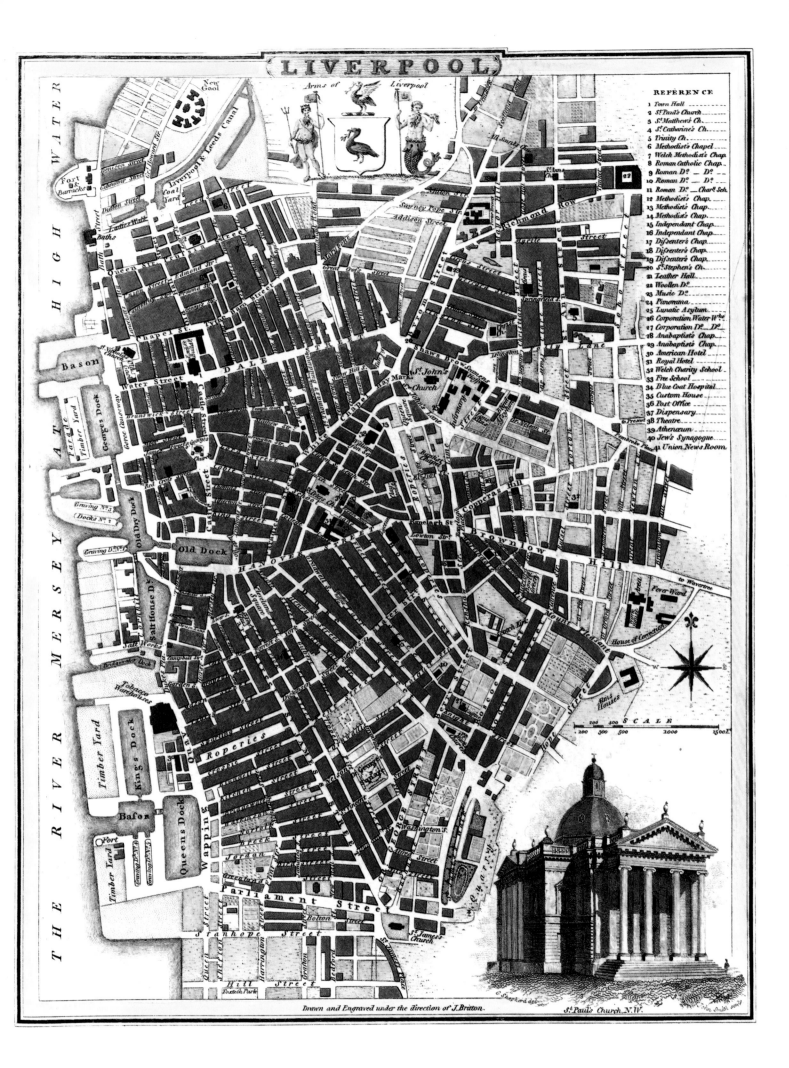

# LIVERPOOL.

Arms of Liverpool

THE RIVER MERSEY AT HIGH WATER

SCALE

St Paul's Church. N.W.

Drawn and Engraved under the direction of J. Britton.

PLATE 10

# YORKSHIRE, NORTH RIDING

### Thomas Moule

*The English Counties Delineated,* 1837

The largest county of England, Yorkshire lies on the North Sea and is bounded by the counties of Durham, Westmoreland, Lancaster, Chester, Derby, Nottingham and Lincoln. It is about 120 miles in its greatest length and 90 in its extreme breadth. It consists of two highlands divided from each other by the Ouse and its tributaries. That on the west has heights of from 2,000 to nearly 3,000 feet above the sea. The other is of a lower elevation, but its sea-cliffs are lofty and steep, and inland it is sometimes above 1,000 feet above the sea. The rivers are the Ouse, the Swale, the Wharfe, the Derwent, the Aire, the Don and the Humber. Coal, iron, building- and limestone are found abundantly. The county is very fertile, and produces in great plenty corn of all kinds; and there are excellent pastures, where cattle, sheep and horses are reared in abundance. Its manufactures are various and most valuable; the iron-works are numerous, and all kinds of cutlery and hardware, all kinds of cloth, woollen and cotton goods and silks are made in vast quantities. The trade of this extensive and populous district is carried on by means of numerous canals and railways, communicating with all parts of the kingdom, and by the port of Hull, on the Humber, with foreign parts. York is its capital city, but there are many other places of great importance. Yorkshire is divided into three parts, called the North, West and East Ridings; and another smaller division is the ainsty of the city of York. The population of North Riding is 204,122, of West Riding 1,154,101, of East Riding, 194,936; of the entire county, 1,591,480. It returns 37 members to Parliament.

### YORK

*For a description and town*

*plan of the city, see Plate 11, pages 30–31.*

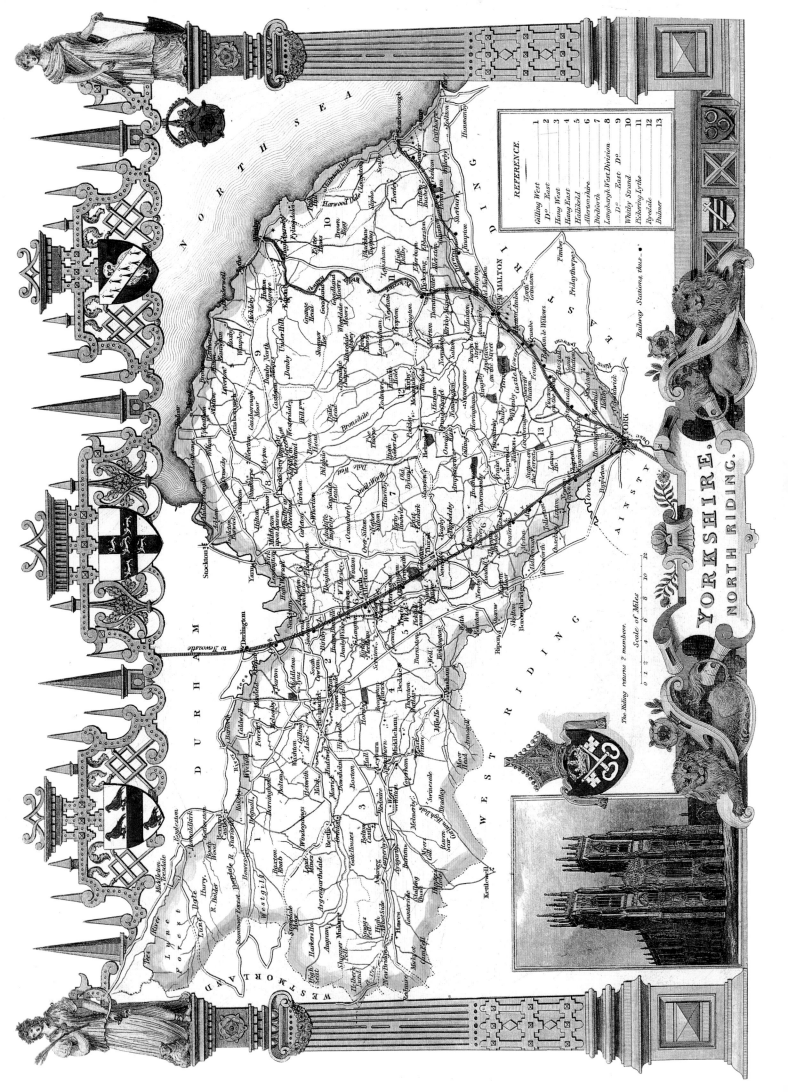

# YORKSHIRE,
## NORTH RIDING.

Railway Stations, thus ......... ■

The Riding returns 2 members.

Scale of Miles
0 1 2 4 6 8 10 12

NORTH SEA

NORTH RIDING

EAST RIDING

WEST RIDING

AINSTY

DURHAM

WESTMORLAND

to Newcastle

York

PLATE 11

# YORK

## John Tallis

*Index-Gazetteer of the World...Illustrated with Plans of*
*the Principal Towns in Great Britain, America etc. Drawn and*
*Engraved from the Most Recent Government Surveys,*
*and Other Authentic Documents, c. 1855*

This city in Yorkshire stands on Watling Street, on the River Ouse at the influx of the Foss, and at a divergence of railways in five directions. It was a centre of Roman roads, which came to it in five directions; it is now a centre of railway communication, from London to Edinburgh, and from coast to coast; it commands sea-ward navigation by the Ouse, and very extensive inland navigation through the Ouse's connections.

The city's structure, till about the commencement of the present century, was remarkably antique and singular; and, notwithstanding numerous and sweeping changes which have been made upon it, it still presents a striking mixture of ancient features with modern ones.

Commerce has never been so extensive as the facilities for export might have made it, and is now less than formerly. A considerable trade is done in drugs, tea, coffee and confectionery. The general retail trade is very large. The manufacture of linens was at one time flourishing, but fell away. The making of combs, gloves, shoes, saddlery and glass is considerable, and there are roperies, tanneries, breweries and large foundries. The police force, in 1864, comprised 40 men, at an annual cost of £2,592. The crimes committed, in 1863, were 82; the persons apprehended 78.

A general weekly market is held on Saturdays, a cattle market on alternate Tuesdays; a wool market on every Thursday from Lady-day to Michaelmas; a leather market on the first Wednesday of March, June, September and December; fairs on Whit-Monday, July 10, August 12 and November 23; and a horse show during the entire week before Christmas. York is 199 miles from London. The population is 28,842.

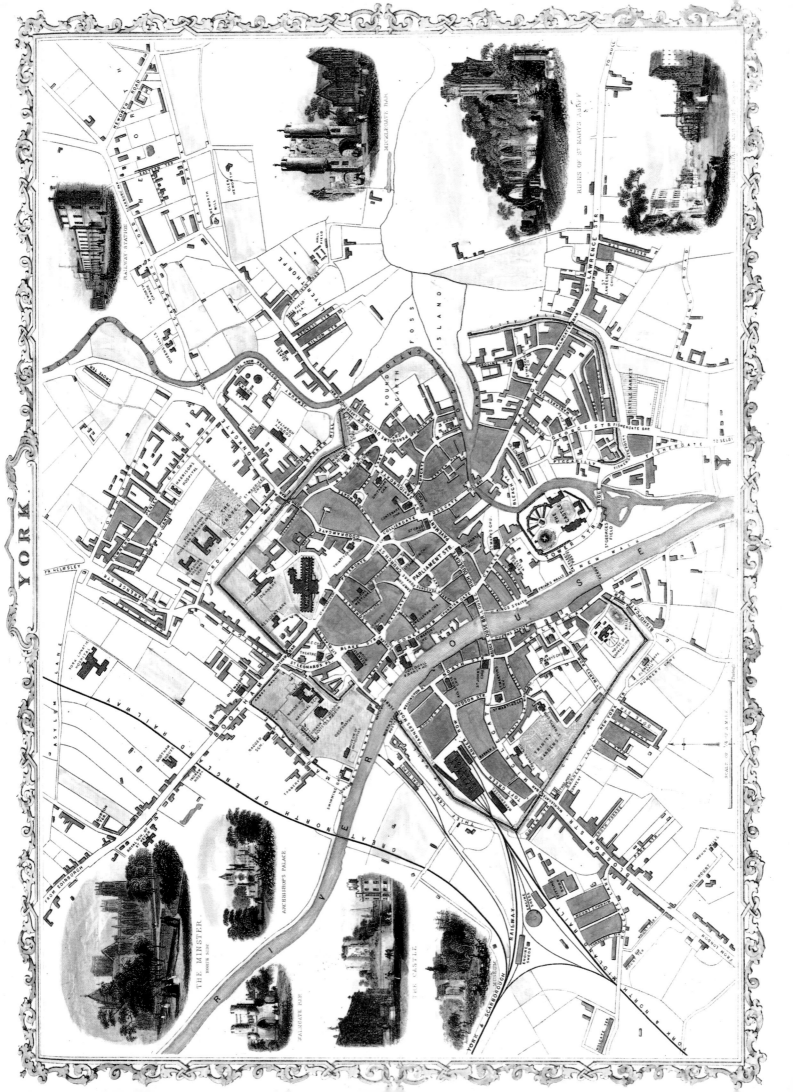

YORK

RAILWAY STATION

MICKLEGATE BAR

RUINS OF ST MARYS ABBEY

THE MINSTER
SOUTH SIDE

ARCHBISHOP'S PALACE

WALMGATE BAR

THE CASTLE

PLATE 12

# YORKSHIRE, WEST RIDING

## Thomas Moule

*The English Counties Delineated,* 1837

### LEEDS

The chief town of the West Riding, Leeds is situated in a vale which trade has rendered one of the most populous spots in England. It is the principal of the clothing towns in Yorkshire, and is a market particularly for the coloured and white broad-cloths, of which vast quantities are sold in its magnificent cloth halls. That called the Mixed-cloth hall is a building of considerable extent, in which the cloth is placed on benches, for sale, every market-day; and the whole business is transacted within little more than an hour, without the least noise or confusion, and with a whisper only, the laws of the market being observed here with particular strictness. The White-cloth hall is a similar building. The factories that supply these two halls lie in the immediate vicinity of the town, on the banks of the rivers. Leeds has a factory of camlets, which has declined, and a flourishing one of carpets, resembling those of Wilts and Scotland. There are also mills for the cutting of tobacco and a great pottery, with several glass-houses. Within three miles of the town are numerous collieries. Of late years the town has been considerably enlarged; and some of the new parts are built, and building, in an elegant style. It is situated on the River Aire, by which it communicates with the Grand Canal. It is 196 miles from London. Markets are held on Tuesdays and Saturdays. The population is 88,741.

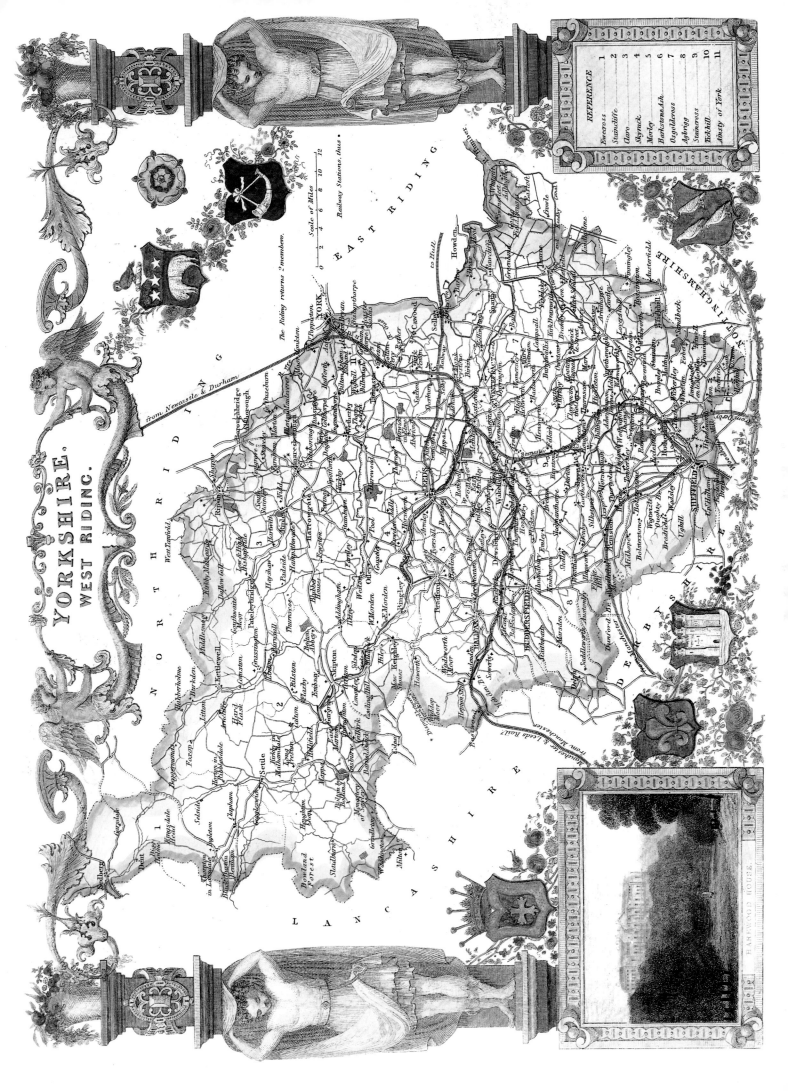

# YORKSHIRE, WEST RIDING.

Scale of Miles

The Riding returns 2 members.

Railway Stations, thus.

EAST RIDING

NORTH RIDING

DERBYSHIRE

NOTTINGHAMSHIRE

LANCASHIRE

HAREWOOD HOUSE.

PLATE 13

# YORKSHIRE, EAST RIDING

## Thomas Moule

*The English Counties Delineated,* 1837

### HULL

The town is seated on a river called the Hull, which rises not far from Driffield and here enters the river Humber. Its situation is extremely advantageous; for, besides its communication with the Yorkshire rivers and canals, it has access also, by the Humber, to the Trent and all its branches and communications. Hence it has the important export trade of many of the northern and midland counties. The foreign trade is chiefly to the Baltic; but it has also a regular traffic with the southern parts of Europe and with America. More ships are sent hence to Greenland than from any other port, that of London excepted. The coasting trade also, for coal, corn, wool and manufactured goods, is very extensive. The harbour is chiefly artificial, consisting of a dock, the largest in the kingdom, with which the river communicates, and in which 800 ships may ride safely and conveniently. Among the public buildings are the Trinity House, for the relief of seamen and their widows; an exchange; and a town-hall. The grand stone bridge over the river to Holderness consists of 14 arches. Hull is 173 miles from London. Markets take place on Tuesdays and Saturdays. The population is 41,629.

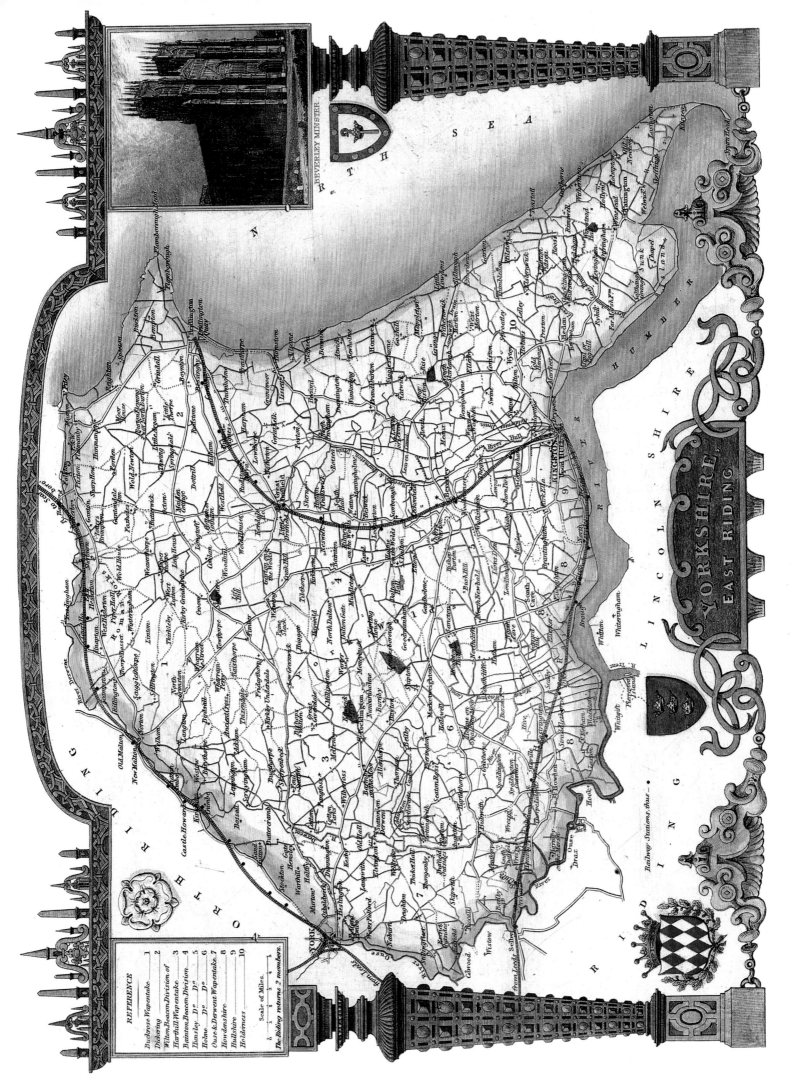

BEVERLEY MINSTER.

## YORKSHIRE, EAST RIDING.

### REFERENCE

| | |
|---|---|
| Buckrose Wapentake | 1 |
| Dickering | 2 |
| Wilton Beacon Division of | 3 |
| Harthill Wapentake | 4 |
| Bainton Beacon Division | 5 |
| Hunsley Do Do | 6 |
| Holme Do Do | 7 |
| Ouse & Derwent Wapentake | 8 |
| Howdenshire | 9 |
| Hullshire | |
| Holderness | 10 |

Scale of Miles

The Riding returns 2 members.

Railway Stations thus ●

NORTH SEA

LINCOLNSHIRE

NORTH RIDING

WEST RIDING

PLATE 14

# CHESHIRE

## Thomas Moule

*The English Counties Delineated,* 1837

A county palatine of England, Cheshire lies on the Irish Sea and is bounded by Lancashire, Yorkshire, Derbyshire, Staffordshire, Shropshire and Wales. It is about 60 miles in length and 30 in breadth. The surface is generally even, but it has some hills. It is watered by the Mersey, the Dee, and the Weaver, with their lesser tributary streams. It has also some great canals and railroads as means of communication. Coal and rock-salt, with some useful kinds of sandstone, are found here; and the salt is a very important feature in the wealth of the county. Dairy-farming is extensively pursued, and much cheese is produced. There is some manufacturing industry, principally on the borders of Lancashire, concerned with cotton, silk and woollens. And textiles, with its salt and its cheese, are its exports not only to other parts of the kingdom but all over the world. Cheshire has 101 parishes. Besides its rivers, there are many good-sized lakes. It is also famed for its forests and plantations. Its population is 395,660.

## DEE

The Dee is a river of North Wales and Cheshire, which rises near Pimble Meer, in Merionethshire, crosses the county of Denbigh, separating it from Cheshire, and runs into the Irish Channel, about 15 miles north-west of Chester. It is navigable from near Ellesmere in Shropshire to Chester.

## CHESTER

*For a description and town*

*plan of the city, see Plate 15, pages 38-39.*

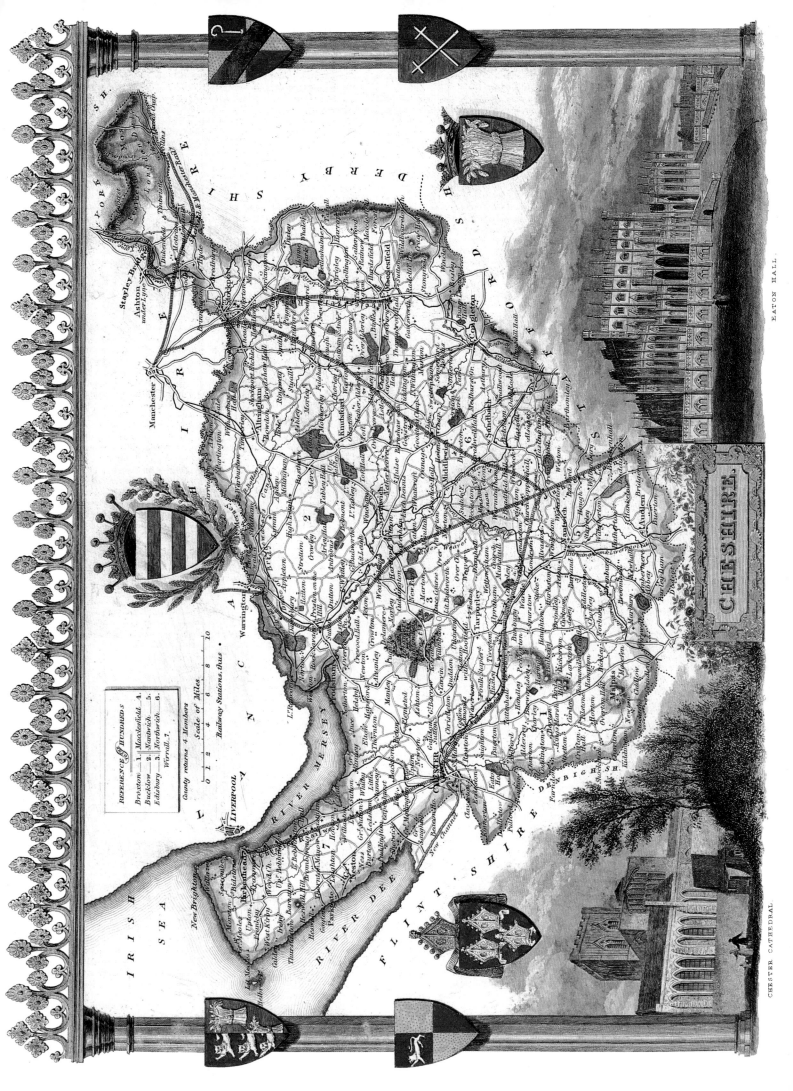

CHESHIRE.

EATON HALL.

CHESTER CATHEDRAL.

REFERENCE to the HUNDREDS
Broxton ___ 1. Macclesfield ___ 4.
Bucklow ___ 2. Nantwich ___ 5.
Eddisbury ___ 3. Northwich ___ 6.
Wirrall ___ 7.

County returns 4 Members

Scale of Miles

Railway Stations, thus

PLATE 15

# CHESTER

## G. Cole and J. Roper

*The British Atlas: Comprising a Complete Set of*
*County Maps of England and Wales; with a General Map of*
*Navigable Rivers and Canals; and Plans of Cities*
*and Principal Towns,* 1801 and later.

The county town of Cheshire, Chester is a large and ancient city, half encircled by a sweep of the River Dee, hence its Roman name of Deva. This name was subsequently relinquished for that of 'Cestria' from Castrium, a military station. The walls of the present city determine the limits of the ancient walls and even the buildings are disposed in the form of a Roman camp, consisting principally of four streets running from a common centre to the cardinal points of the compass. These streets have been excavated from a stratum of rock, and in consequence are sunken several feet below the natural surface, a circumstance which has produced a singular construction of the houses. On the level of the street are low shops and warehouses, and above them a gallery on each side reaching from street to street open in front and balustraded. These galleries, called 'rows', appear exceedingly curious to strangers, as they seem to be formed through the first floors of the houses.

Chester may be deemed a sort of provincial metropolis for the gentry of the neighbouring counties of moderate fortune. Its maritime trade is chiefly coasting and with Ireland, whence great quantities of linen are imported. Besides linen, wood, hides, tallow, feathers, butter, provisions and other articles are received from Ireland; grocery from London, timber from Wales; hemp, flax and iron from the Baltic; and fruit, oil, barilla, cork and wine from Spain and Portugal. The exports are coal, lead, calomine, copper-plates, cast-iron and vast quantities of cheese. The only manufacture of any consequence is that of gloves. Annual races commencing on the first Monday in May are run on the Roodeye, a fine level course beneath the city walls, from which the races are to be seen to great advantage. The town is 183 miles from London. The population is 19,949.

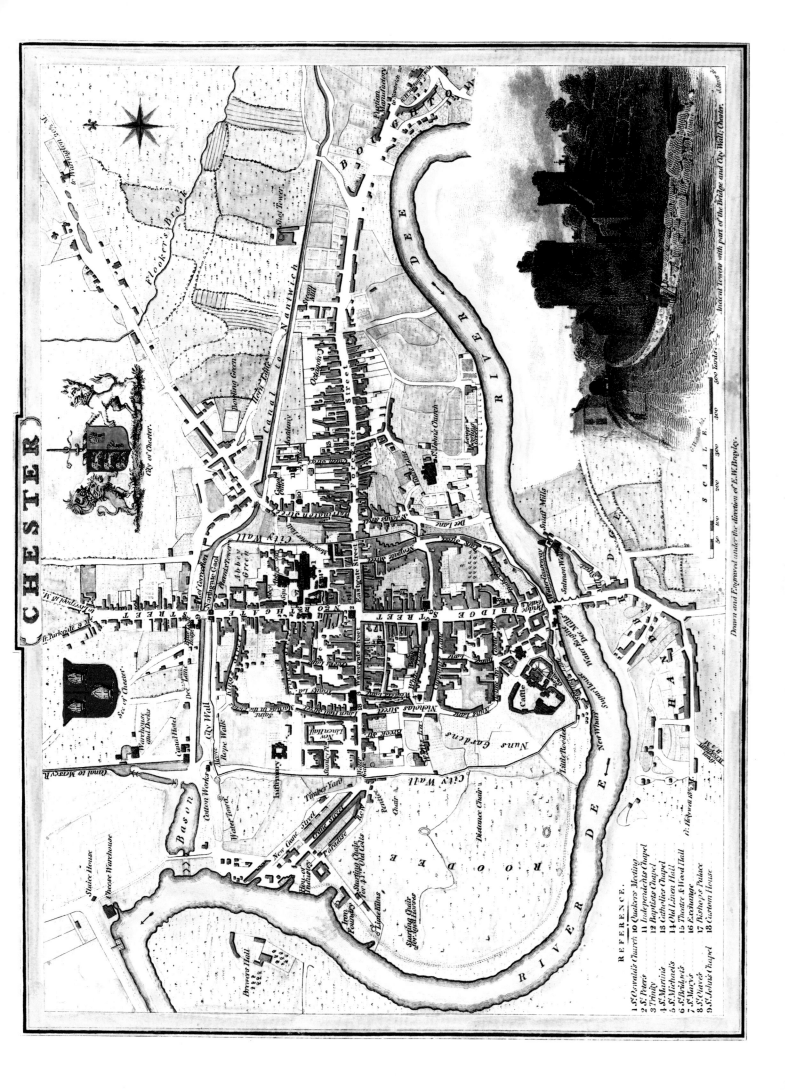

# CHESTER

**REFERENCE.**

1. St. Oswald's Church
2. St. Peter's
3. Trinity
4. St. Martin's
5. St. Michael's
6. St. Bridget's
7. St. Mary's
8. St. Olave's
9. St. John's Chapel
10. Quakers Meeting
11. Independents Chapel
12. Baptists Chapel
13. Catholic Chapel
14. Old Linen Hall
15. Theatre & Wool Hall
16. Exchange
17. Bishop's Palace
18. Custom House

Drawn and Engraved under the direction of E. W. Brayley.

Ancient Towers with part of the Bridge and City Walls, Chester.

PLATE 16

# DERBYSHIRE

## Thomas Moule

### *The English Counties Delineated,* 1837

A county of England, Derbyshire is bounded by Cheshire, Staffordshire, Yorkshire, Nottinghamshire, Leicestershire and Warwickshire. It extends nearly 56 miles in length from north to south and 34 from east to west where broadest; but in the south part it is not above six. The north and west parts are mountainous, some heights being nearly 2,000 feet above the sea. The south and east parts are fertile, producing most kinds of grain, particularly barley. The mountains abound in the best lead, with marble, alabaster, mill-stones, iron, coal and a coarse sort of crystal. There is good pasture in the valleys. Some important manufacturing industry is carried on in this county. The principal rivers are the Derwent, Dove, Erwash and Trent. It returns six members to Parliament. The population numbers 272,217.

## DERWENT

A river of Derbyshire, the Derwent rises in the High Peak and after passing through the county falls into the Trent eight miles from Derby. The same name is given to a river of Yorkshire which rises in the North Riding and runs south to fall into the Ouse five miles south-east of Selby; also to a river of Durham, flowing through a romantic tract of county and falling into the Tyne, a little above Newcastle, near which, on its banks, are some capital iron-works. Finally, there is a River Derwent in Cumberland, which rises in Borrowdale, flows through Derwent-Water and Bassingthwaite-Water, passes by Cockermouth and falls into the Irish Sea at Workington.

## DERBY

*For a description and town*

*plan of the city, see Plate 17, pages 42-43.*

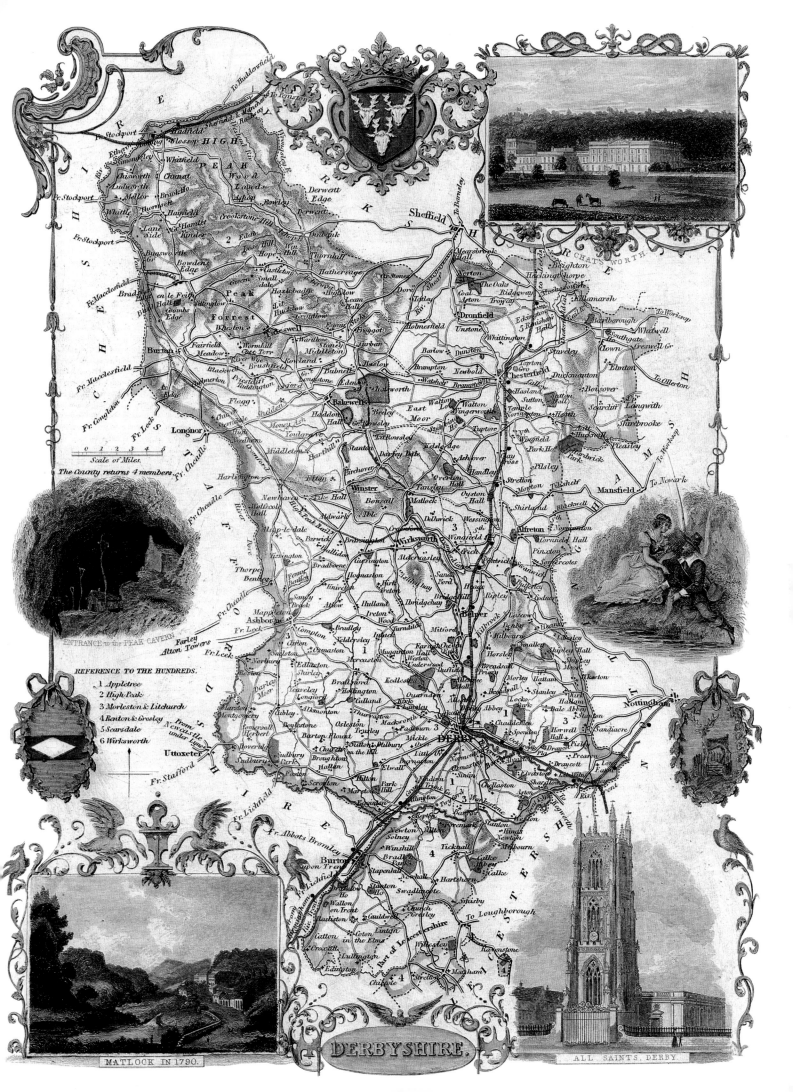

ENTRANCE to the PEAK CAVERN

REFERENCE TO THE HUNDREDS.
1 Appletree
2 High Peak
3 Morleston & Litchurch
4 Renton & Gresley
5 Scarsdale
6 Wirksworth

The County returns 4 members.

Scale of Miles.

CHATSWORTH

DERBYSHIRE.

MATLOCK IN 1790.

ALL SAINTS, DERBY.

PLATE 17

# DERBY

## G. Cole and J. Roper

*The British Atlas: Comprising a Complete Set of
County Maps of England and Wales; with a General Map of
Navigable Rivers and Canals; and Plans of Cities
and Principal Towns,* 1801 and later.

The county town of Derbyshire, Derby comprises many handsome houses of modern erection as well as some good public buildings. The streets are spacious and well paved, and through a considerable part of the town flows a stream called Markerton Brook, over which there are five stone bridges. Among the principal public edifices are the Assembly Room on the east of the marketplace, erected by subscription in about 1774, and the Guildhall built by the Corporation in about 1730. A free-school has been founded here at which the celebrated astronomer Flamstead is said to have been educated. The Derbyshire General Infirmary is one of the noblest structures of the kind in England, completed for the reception of patients in 1800, at an expense of £17,870 including the price paid for the ground on which it stands. This place was formerly a great wool-mart; and the art of dyeing woollen cloth was supposed to be practised here with particular advantage, in consequence of the water of the Derwent being especially adapted for that purpose.

Derby ale is mentioned by Camden in the reign of Elizabeth, and a century later the town retained its reputation for making malt and malt liquor. It has long been famous for its silk-works. In 1814 there were ten in the town, affording employment to about 1,200 persons. The porcelain manufacture was introduced in about 1750 and the articles produced are said to surpass the finest of foreign workmanship. Fluorspar, marble and alabaster are here manufactured into a variety of articles, useful and ornamental. Derby is 126 miles from London. The population numbers 10,728.

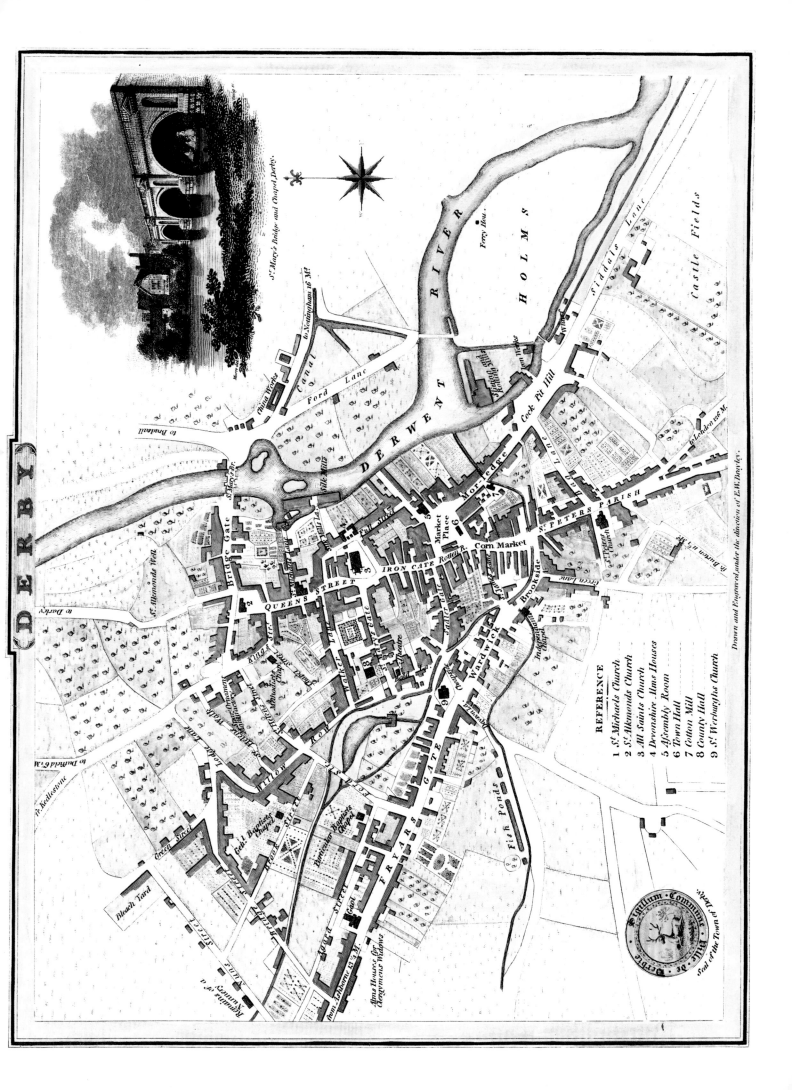

DERBY

St Mary's Bridge and Chapel Derby.

REFERENCE
1 St Michaels Church
2 St Alkmonds Church
3 All Saints Church
4 Devonshire Alms Houses
5 Assembly Room
6 Town Hall
7 Cotton Mill
8 County Hall
9 St Werburghs Church

Drawn and Engraved under the direction of E.W.Brayley.

SIGILLVM · COMMVNE · VILLE · DE · DERBIE
Seal of the Town of Derby.

RIVER

HOLMS

Castle Fields

Siddals Lane

DERWENT

Ferry Hou

Cock Pit Hill

to London 126 M.

to Burton 11 1/2 M.

St Peters Parish

St Peters Church

Green Lane

Brookside

Independant Chapel

Corn Market

Market Place

Morledge

Iron Gate

Queens Street

Bridge Gate

St Alkmonds Well

to Nottingham 16 M.

Canal

Ford Lane

China Works

to Bradsall

Silk Mills

St Mary's Chr

Fish Ponds

Willow Row

King's St.

Walker Lane

Friars Gate

Bold Lane

Theatre

Warwick

Nuns St

Bridgegate

Gaol

Gaol Street

Agard Street

from Ashborne 13 1/2 M.

Alms Houses for Clergymens Widows

Genl Baptists Chapel

Particular Baptists Chapel

Bleach Yard

Green Street

to Duffd 6 1/2 M.

to Kedleston

to Derby

Bridge Fields

Markeaton Walk

St Michaels Church

St Helens Walk

PLATE 18

# NOTTINGHAMSHIRE

## Thomas Moule

### *The English Counties Delineated,* 1837

Nottinghamshire is a county of England, bounded by Yorkshire, Lincolnshire, Leicestershire and Derbyshire. Its greatest length is 50 miles, its greatest breadth about 25. It contains 13 towns and 168 parishes. The principal rivers are the Trent and Idle. Almost the whole of the middle and western parts of the county were formerly occupied by the extensive forest of Sherwood, which is the only royal forest north of the Trent; but the wood has in many parts been cleared, and the extent of the forest has been greatly reduced. The chief products of this county are corn, malt and pitcoal, of which there is great plenty. Other commodities include malt, wool, liquorice, wood, fish and fowl. Manufactured goods chiefly consist of frame-work, knitting, glass and earthenware. The population is 249,910.

## NOTTINGHAM

Nottingham is pleasantly situated on a rocky eminence above the meadows bordering the Trent. On the highest part stands the castle, a large, elegant and noble palace belonging to the Duke of Newcastle, with a most extensive prospect. Nottingham is a large, populous and handsome town, with a spacious market-place. It is considered one of the principal seats of stocking manufacture, particularly of the finer kinds, such as those of silk and cotton. Nottingham also has a factory of glass and coarse earthenware, and a considerable trade in malt. It is remarkable for its vaults or cellars cut in the rock. It is 125 miles from London. Markets are held on Wednesdays and Saturdays, and fairs on the Friday after January 13, May 7, the Thursday before Easter and October 2. The population is 53,091.

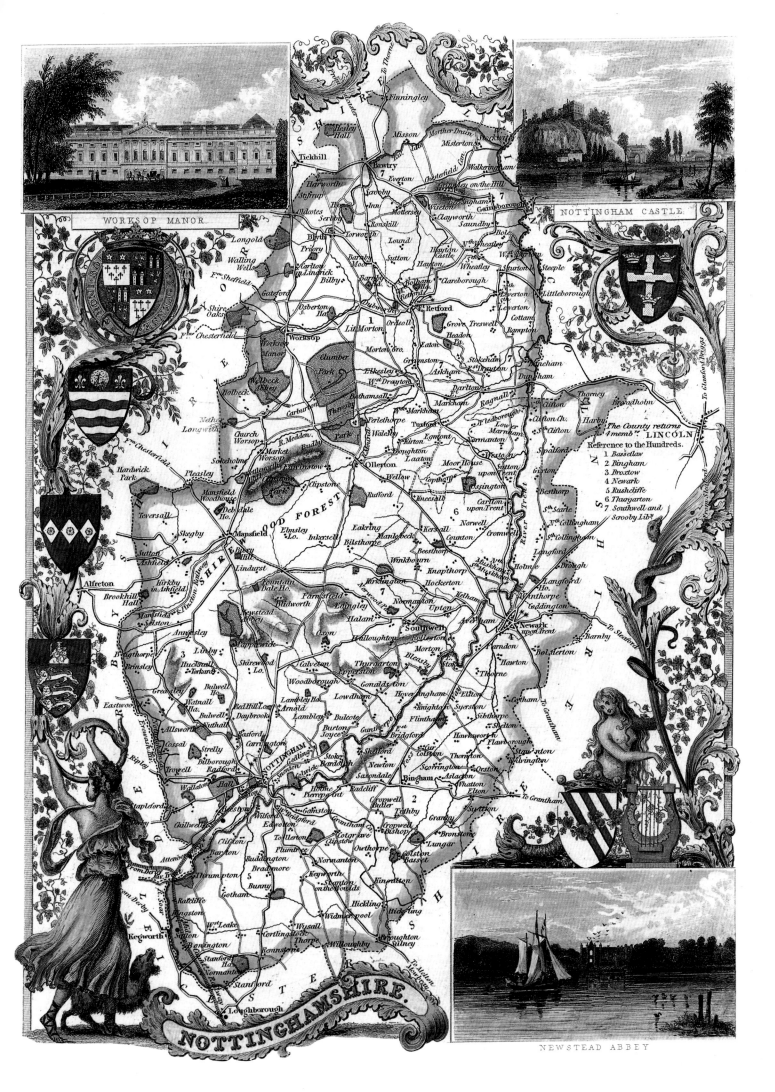

WORKSOP MANOR.

NOTTINGHAM CASTLE.

NEWSTEAD ABBEY

NOTTINGHAMSHIRE.

The County returns
4 memb LINCOLN
Reference to the Hundreds.
1 Bassetlaw
2 Bingham
3 Broxtow
4 Newark
5 Rushcliffe
6 Thurgarton
7 Southwell and
Scrooby Libᵗʸ

PLATE 19

# LINCOLNSHIRE

## Thomas Moule

### *The English Counties Delineated,* 1837

Lincolnshire is a county of England, lying on the German Ocean and bounded by Norfolk, Cambridgeshire, Northamptonshire, Rutland, Leicestershire, Nottinghamshire and Yorkshire. It is 77 miles in length and 48 in breadth at its widest. It is divided into three parts, namely Holland on the south-east, Kesteven on the south-west and Lindsey on the north. It contains one city, 33 market towns and 630 parishes. Its principal rivers are the Trent, Humber, Witham, Welland, Ancam, Nen and Dun. The air is various, according to its three grand divisions. The soil in many places is very rich, the inland part producing corn in great plenty, and the fens cole-seed and very rich pastures, whence their breed of cattle is larger than that of any other county in England except Somersetshire. Their horses are also excellent and very large; and their sheep are not only of the largest breed, but are clothed with a long thick wool, peculiarly fitted for worsted and coarse woollen manufactures. The county has some manufacturing industry also. The population is 362,602. It sends 13 members to Parliament.

## LINCOLN

Lincoln was formerly called Nicol. This city is pleasantly situated on the side of a hill, on the Witham, which here divides itself into three small channels. It is much reduced from its former extent and splendour (when it contained 52 parish churches, and was one of the most populous cities of England and a market for all goods coming by land or water) and now consists principally of one street, above two miles long, well paved, and several cross and parallel streets well peopled. Here are some handsome modern buildings, but more antique ones. The Romans' northgate still remains under the name of Newport Gate. It is a vast semicircle of stones, of very large dimensions, laid without mortar and connected only by their uniform shape. The cathedral is a stately Gothic pile, one of the largest in England, and stands on so lofty a hill, that it may be seen 50 miles to the north and 30 to the south. It is particularly admired for its interior architecture, which is in the richest and lightest Gothic style. The famous bell, called Tom of Lincoln, is surpassed in magnitude by only two others in England. The chief trade here is in coals brought by the Trent and Fossdyke; and oats and wool, which are sent by the river Witham. The city is 129 miles from London. Markets are held on Tuesdays and Fridays. The population numbers 16,172.

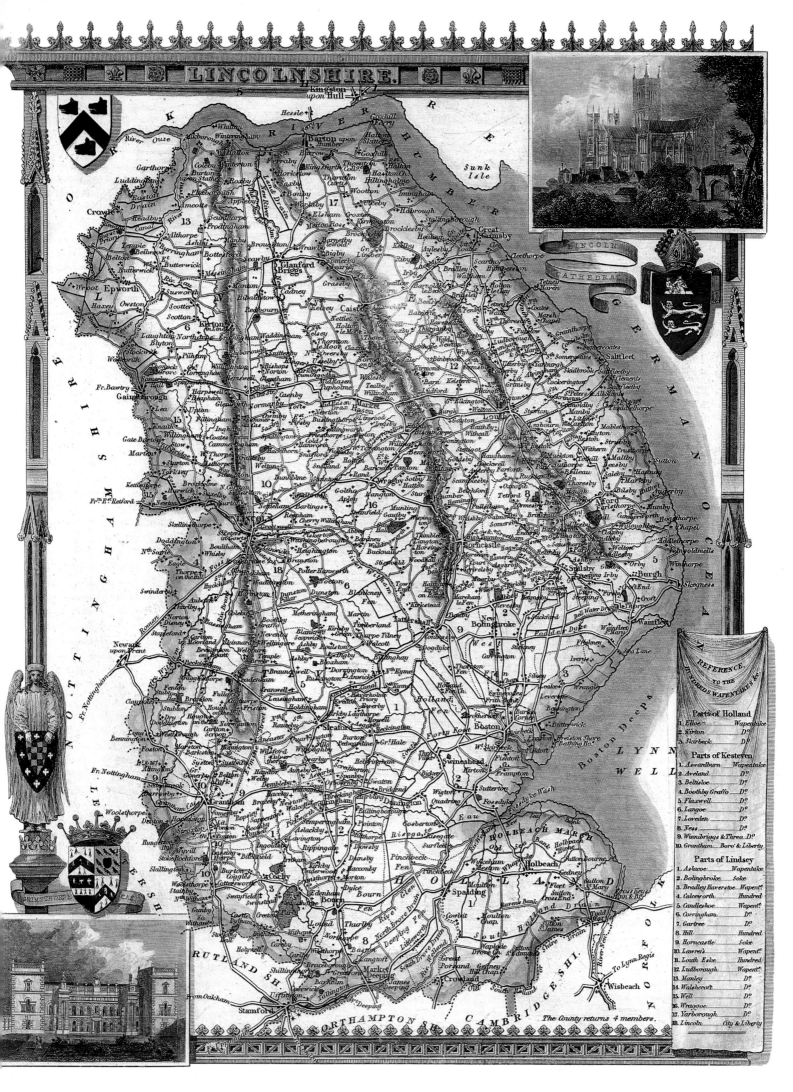

# LINCOLNSHIRE.

LINCOLN CATHEDRAL

The County returns 4 members.

# LIST OF ILLUSTRATIONS

# BIBLIOGRAPHY

The local descriptions accompanying the plates in this book have been compiled from the following sources:

Barclay, James, *Barclay's Complete and Universal Dictionary*, London, 1842.

Britton, John and Brayley, Edward, *The Beauties of England and Wales*, London, 1801-1818.

Gorton, John, *Topographical Dictionary of Great Britain and Ireland*, London, 1831-1833.

Lewis, Samuel, *Topographical Dictionary of England*, London, 1831.

Lewis, Samuel, *Topographical Dictionary of Ireland*, London, 1837.

Lewis, Samuel, *Topographical Dictionary of Scotland*, London, 1837.

Smith, David, *Victorian Maps of the British Isles*, London, 1985.

Tallis, John, *Tallis's Topographical Dictionary of England and Wales*, London, *c.* 1860.

Wilson, John Marius, *The Imperial Gazetteer of England and Wales*, London, 1866-1869.